Zur freundlichen Erinnerung
an eine zu kurze gemeinsame Zeit
in New York

Weihnachten 1989

[signature]

THE FACE OF NEW YORK

Also by Andreas Feininger:

FEININGER ON PHOTOGRAPHY
ADVANCED PHOTOGRAPHY
SUCCESSFUL PHOTOGRAPHY
SUCCESSFUL COLOR PHOTOGRAPHY

Also by Susan E. Lyman:

ONE HUNDRED NEW YORK YEARS. 1848–1948

THE FACE

OF

NEW YORK

THE CITY AS IT WAS AND AS IT IS

Photographs by ANDREAS FEININGER
Life staff photographer

Text by SUSAN E. LYMAN
Museum of the City of New York

CROWN PUBLISHERS, INC. • NEW YORK

All the photographs in this book, unless otherwise designated, were taken by *Life* photographer, Andreas Feininger. Those originally published in *Life* are copyrighted by Time, Inc., whom the authors and publishers thank for allowing their use in these pages.

Third Printing, October, 1957

Manufactured in U. S. A.
American Book–Stratford Press, Inc., New York

I wish to offer sincere thanks to John Walden Myer, Director of the Museum of the City of New York, and to my colleagues on the Staff for their interest; I am particularly grateful to Miss Grace M. Mayer, Curator of Prints at the Museum of the City of New York, who has been of the greatest help through her vast knowledge of the material available and by her continued support and advice during the preparation of this book. Special thanks go, also, to R. W. G. Vail, Director of the New York Historical Society, for the use of pictures from their rich collections, to the *Daily News,* and to Fairchild Aerial Surveys, Inc., for photographs supplied by them.

SUSAN E. LYMAN

New York City is big in every way: masses of buildings, multitudes of people, and an incredible amount of activity. Things here are counted not singly, but by hundreds and thousands. This bigness which might well, by its ponderousness, have a stifling effect on anything as small as the individual living here has, instead, the opposite effect. It produces vehement feeling. How often do you hear the remarks, "I wouldn't live in New York if you gave it to me," and conversely, "I wouldn't live anywhere else." How rarely you hear a middle-of-the-road, unemotional comment. Everyone has convictions about New York.

Here, then, is the New York of Andreas Feininger, the convictions of a great photographer. For years he has explored the city, searching with his camera for the facets that to him mean New York and, through the medium of his extraordinary photography, capturing these to produce the face of his New York.

First of all, there are the skyscrapers, which for him have a savage quality, a reversion to the prehistoric that is unique among cities. Paradoxically, as the buildings have become giants, so the people have become infinitesimal, completely dominated, he feels, by the structures they have created. Yet the people themselves interest him strongly and he wanders among them, thinking of the many countries they came from, looking at their home surroundings and their daily activities. A part of the city for which he has a particular fondness is the waterfront, with its infinite variety of activity—and he watches the crowds pouring from a ferry boat, the heaving crane swinging a locomotive high into the air, and a superliner gently nosing into her berth.

Having established his modern New York, Mr. Feininger then turned to the past, to see what influences had shaped his city, what physical changes such as buildings and parks had affected certain streets and areas. At the Museum of the City of New York he found the answer in many different forms, perhaps captured by Eliza Greatorex's romantic pen or Jacob Riis's crusading camera; maybe a scene engraved by an unknown artist two centuries ago or a detail photographed by Percy Byron in 1900.

By this time I was working along with Mr. Feininger, trying to bring 350 years of New York history into focus with this picture of the present city. After a final choice of material was made, to me fell the pleasant task of attempting to tell the history behind each picture, to tie in the unfamiliar past with the well-known present. All of us are aware of bits and pieces of city history. Yes, we know it was once a Dutch town, but we aren't sure how much area it covered then. We've read of the Crystal Palace but have no idea where it stood. Maybe we've been lucky enough to hear an old-timer describe the building of Brooklyn Bridge or the rigors of an immigrant's arrival at Castle Garden—but we've not seen pictures of these events. Here, in this book, you'll be able to fit together some of these pieces of history. You'll be able to link the old and the new—a very satisfying thing to do because history is that third dimension which brings depth to any scene of the present.

Finally, looking ahead to the next time that you ramble through the city, I hope that you will recollect some of the pictures you've looked at in this book. For instance, the next time you stop by Rockefeller Center, may you see not only the ice-skaters on the Lower Plaza but also the visitors to Dr. Hosack's Elgin Botanic Garden. As you walk along 42nd past the towering Chrysler and *Daily News* Buildings, may you see also the cluster of shanties that stood there in the 1860's. And, best of all, as you fly over the city, may you see not only the skyscrapers and the pattern of streets, but also the open green countryside of Manhattan Island with the small Dutch village at the tip, for this is all part and parcel of our New York.

SUSAN ELIZABETH LYMAN

The Pictures

In compiling the material for this book, the most important considerations were those of selection and presentation—what to show, and how to show it.

To assemble a complete pictorial record of a city the size of New York is physically impossible. In addition to its prohibitive size and cost, any such volume would also be rather boring, since so many aspects of a city, no matter how important to its proper functioning, are so familiar to the average reader that he has no desire to see them reproduced in the form of photographs.

Furthermore, the appearance of public buildings such as railroad stations, post offices, court houses, theatres, museums, libraries, etc., is so standardized throughout the world that they look more or less the same, whether they are located in New York, London, Cape Town, or Hongkong. No matter how indispensable to the civic and cultural life of a city, such buildings are not typical of New York, and consequently, photographs of such stereotyped subjects have been deliberately omitted in favor of more significant views.

More than most other cities, New York abounds with interesting features because it possesses three distinct qualities: located at the junction of an ocean and a continent, it is the world's biggest city; it is built on an island; and it has the longest waterfront of any city on earth.

The repercussions of this are threefold:

New York's immense size attracts from all points of the globe initiative, talent, and wealth which, directly or indirectly, have created such spectacular achievements as Rockefeller Center, the Empire State and United Nations Buildings, Wall Street, Fifth Avenue, and other equally exciting features.

Because its island location limited New York's horizontal expansion, the city was forced to grow upward. This fact was primarily responsible for the evolvement of that typical American symbol, the skyscraper, which has nowhere attained such spectacular dimensions as in New York, culminating in the famous skyline.

And finally, thanks to its 770 miles of sheltered waterfront, New York possesses not only the largest, but also one of the finest harbors on earth. As a result, New York has direct sea-connection with some thirty foreign countries and access to commerce with the entire world.

My main consideration in assembling the illustrations for this book was to do justice to these and other aspects of the city which unmistakably spell "New York."

However, no matter how carefully selected and how typical of New York, unless presented in a photographically effective form, even the most interesting subjects become meaningless and dull.

For example, seen from almost anywhere along Fifth Avenue (where it is located), the Empire State Building, the tallest structure in the world, for reasons of perspective appears lower than most of the actually much smaller skyscrapers that happen to be closer to the observer. No photograph taken from any such viewpoint, of course, gives a true impression of this spectacular building, which can only be fully appreciated when seen from a distance. Similarly, only when seen from an adequate distance does New York's magnificent skyline appear at its monumental best. The closer the viewpoint, the more do relatively low but nearby buildings hide the taller but more distant structures that line the backbone of Manhattan, the less does one see of the skyline, and the less interesting do the photographs appear. To counteract these deceptive effects of "perspective," the author, whenever possible, took his pictures from a distance with the aid of a telephoto lens.

In this connection, it seems necessary to point out that, contrary to often-encountered opinion, telephoto lenses do *not* produce pictures in which perspective is "distorted." Such photographs may appear unusual and surprising, but as far as perspective is concerned, they are no more "distorted" than pictures taken with ordinary lenses. This can be verified easily: take a number of photographs of the same subject from the same camera point of view, but with lenses of different focal length (wide-angle, standard, or telephoto). *If enlarged to the same scale*, the photographs may differ in sharpness and definition as a result of their different degrees of enlargement, but *they are identical as far as perspective is concerned*. The area encompassed by the lens, of course, may vary, but within this area, line for line and angle for angle, perspective will be found to be the same, and the pictures will register perfectly if superimposed one upon the other.

Telephotographs render in picture form a view as it would appear to the eye if seen through a pair of binoculars. They depict only a comparatively narrow angle of a scene, but render this section in a scale large enough to show detail that from the camera point of view cannot be distinguished by the eye because it is too far away. Since they show the subject in a form which differs from that in which we saw it when we took the picture, telephotographs may seem unusual. However, this quality, far from being a type of "distortion," actually represents a form of intensified seeing. Used in this sense—as a means for extending our visual experience—the telephoto lens helps us to see more clearly subjects as they truly are, freed from the misleading chance-effects of "perspective." As mentioned before, photographed from close by with an ordinary lens, the Empire State Building appears less tall than buildings which are actually lower but nearer. This apparent smallness, which is caused by perspective and which is contrary to fact, is in effect a form of distortion. On the other hand, in telephotographs taken from farther away, the Empire State Building rises monumentally above its lower neighbors. Because telephotographs come closer than pictures taken with an ordinary lens to preserving the true proportions of the subject, they create impressions which conform more closely to reality. This makes telephotographs the more effective type of picture.

For similar reasons, the author, as far as possible, utilized other typically photographic qualities in order to depict effectively his vast subject, New York. To mention one more example: in black-and-white photography, color, of course, cannot be rendered directly (as in a color photograph), but must be represented in the form of different shades of gray. Because of the various controls which a photographer has over his medium, this can be done in several ways. The common approach to the problem of color translation into terms of black and white is to match brightness of color and gray shade. But such a "literal" approach has one serious disadvantage: in reality, colors of equal brightness appear separated because of differences in hue; transformed into corresponding shades of gray, however, colors different in hue but equal in brightness appear as identical gray tones; differentiation is absent, and objects merge one into another. To avoid this, the author, with the aid of color filters, transformed color values into degrees of contrast, and "symbolized" the color effect of his subjects by means of stark and "graphic" black and white.

All the New York City photographs taken by the author were made on Kodak Super XX Film; exposed in accordance with readings taken from a Weston exposure meter; processed in Kodak Developer D-76; and enlarged on glossy Kodabromide Paper developed in Kodak Developer D-72. Three different cameras were used: for the close-ups, a twin-lens reflex camera 2¼″ x 2¼″; for the medium-long shots, a single-lens reflex camera of the same size in conjunction with telephoto lenses of different focal lengths; and for the long shots, a specially constructed 4″ x 5″ view-type camera and lenses with focal lengths up to 43″.

The author also made all the reproductions of historical photographs, lithographs, and engravings used in this book. While engaged in this work, he was struck by the excellent state of preservation of the engravings—many of them two and three hundred years old—as compared to the poor condition of photographs taken only fifty to seventy-five years ago. While the paper of the engravings still appeared white and crisp, and the lines sharp and black, most of the photographs were already faded, yellow, and seemed destined to complete obliteration within a relatively short time—eloquent testimony to the impermanence of our present methods of graphic representation. The reproductions of the old photographs in this book appear relatively contrasty only because of modern techniques of copying which, to a certain extent, permit restoration of the contrast of the faded original.

Another fact which greatly impressed the author was the high degree of skill and the attention to detail with which most of the old engravings and lithographs were executed. As a result, small sections of old prints could be photographed and enlarged without noticeable loss of detail. Several unusual and significant pictures were produced in this manner.

All copy-work was done on Kodak Plus-X Film 4" x 5", developed in Kodak Developer D-76, and, in accordance with the requirements of the reproduction, printed on Kodabromide Paper of medium or hard gradation.

ANDREAS FEININGER

THE FACE OF NEW YORK

NOVI BELGII
NOVÆQVE ANGLIÆ NEC NON
PARTIS
VIRGINIÆ TABULA
multis in locis emendata a
Hugo Allardt

NIEUW AMSTERDAM.
Op 't Eylandt Manhattans.

J. Clarence Davies Collection, Museum of the City of New York

The towers of Manhattan, the heart of the great city, make a magnificent panorama from the New Jersey heights. With this first glimpse you see the true New York, that giant of steel and stone, unlike any other place in the world, which millions of people claim as their home, where hundreds of thousands more spend their working hours.

What has given New York the qualities that are as distinctive as the buildings themselves? What about the multitudes who live here? How has it grown since those days when it was the Dutch town of New Amsterdam and the slowly turning arms of a windmill were the outstanding sight on the horizon?

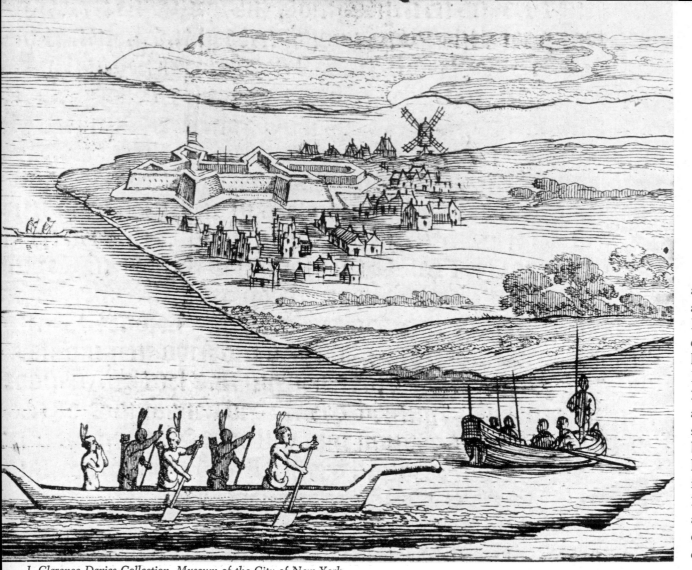

Thirty houses and a windmill grouped around a fort: that was New Amsterdam according to the earliest known picture, "The Hartgers View," 1626–28. The first settlers had arrived from Holland several years before, had bought Manhattan Island from the Indians in 1626, and were now 200 strong and getting a good start as a trading colony for the West India Company.

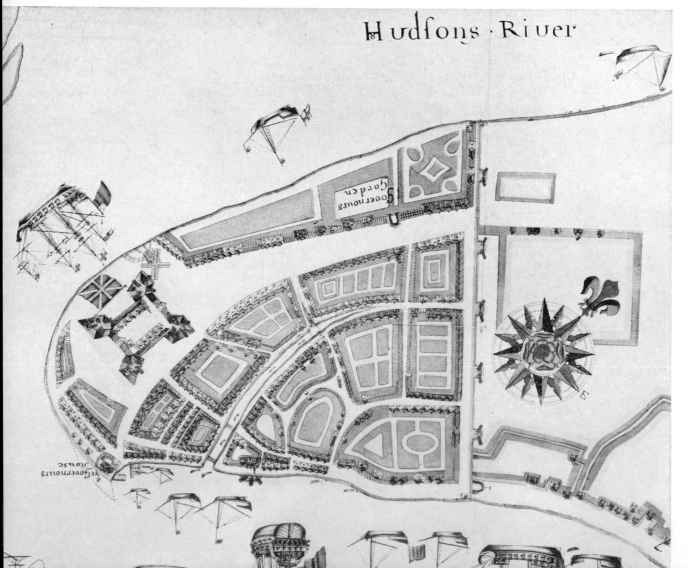

Hudfons · Riuer

By 1664 the town extended to Wall Street and had 1,500 inhabitants. In that year the English forced the town to surrender, claiming prior right to the territory, and named it in honor of the Duke of York. "The Duke's Plan" (left), probably a Dutch-made map, was decorated with English warships and flag and sent to the Duke of York to show him his new holdings.

Fairchild Aerial Surveys, Inc.

Although the town had remained in Dutch hands for only forty years, their influence continued for a century more and even today Dutch "Father Knickerbocker" symbolizes New York. As an English colony it grew steadily, and by 1775, 23,000 people were living south of the present Chambers Street. Then for seven years New York was in enemy hands, serving as British headquarters during the Revolution. After the war the city found itself playing an extremely important part as capital of the state from 1784 to 1796 and as federal capital from 1785 to 1790. Washington was inaugurated president here in April, 1789, and remained until August, 1790, when the capital was transferred to Philadelphia.

It was about this time, 1790, that New York began her extraordinary expansion. By 1850 the built-up area extended to 42nd Street and by 1890 the island was generally covered. With the creation of Greater New York in 1898, Manhattan and the Bronx were joined by Brooklyn, Queens and Staten Island, and the population doubled, jumping to 3,100,000.

Since then the growth has been of another sort as the builders reached up into the sky. But still today you can see where the town began on Manhattan's tip. Around the edges is much "made" land of later date but in the center foreground stands the hollow square of the Custom House, the site of the old fort at the foot of Broadway. This is—and was—New York.

By contrast this view of the city from New Jersey bears absolutely no relation to its past history. There is no hint of the small Dutch village, the growing English colony or the rapidly developing city of the 1800's. This is the twentieth century rising full-grown from the native soil. It is the modern city and it is unmistakably New York, forced by the narrow limits of Manhattan into becoming a city of skyscrapers.

However, it brings a sense of far greater antiquity. At times the modern and the primitive can be very close, and here the skyscrapers rise up like prehistoric monoliths, seemingly the tombstones left by an extinct race of giants. The reaching New York skyline is seen from a distance of about seven miles. The photograph was taken on Route 6 near Bendix, N. J., and the Hudson River lies beyond the ridge.

Afbeeldinge van de stadt Amsterdam in Nieuw Neederlandt.

The original settlement was laid out according to Company instructions from Holland, and by 1660, when the above map was drawn, the town had 300 houses and the pattern of early streets as we know them was established. This only extant plan of New Amsterdam was made here and sent home to the West India Company. Later the original disappeared, but a contemporary copy that had been drawn for the Medici family was found in 1911 in the Medicis' Villa Castello. Hence its name "Castello Plan."

The gray-walled fort dominated the tip of Manhattan for nearly two centuries, and its different names through the years reflect the changing history of the city: beginning with Fort Amsterdam, next Fort James, then Fort Willem Hendrick. The latter was in 1673–74 during that short period when the Dutch held the town a second time and called it New Orange. After fifteen months New Orange was returned by treaty to England again. With the accession of new British rulers, the fort became in turn Fort Anne and then Fort George.

By 1731, when this picture was drawn, Fort George was guarding a prosperous English colony. There was a constantly increasing number of wharves and shipyards; there were coffee houses, theaters, public gardens and stately homes. A new City Hall was completed in Wall Street in 1704; a newspaper, *The New-York Gazette,* appeared in 1725; and a college (Kings, now Columbia) was founded in 1754. There

was even more land, because all along the East River the area was being filled in and Pearl Street, the original water line, was now a block inland and the new Water Street marked the river's edge. (Today the man-made land covers a large area—three blocks on the east, Water, Front and South Streets; Battery Park on the south; and two blocks on the Hudson, Washington and West Streets.)

One of the greatest events during the colonial period was John Peter Zenger's trial in 1736. His courageous stand as editor of *The New York Weekly Journal* resulted in a lawsuit for libel. His acquittal insured freedom of the press and freedom of speech not only in New York but throughout the country. The various churches in this view bear testimony to another liberty, the right to religious freedom that was enjoyed here. Spires and belfries made an imposing array on the horizon and, together with the fort, afforded a fine view for people sailing up the harbor.

Today, as we approach the tip of Manhattan we
are entranced by the imposing sight, no matter
whether it is for the first time or for the hundredth,
whether we are seeing it in the bright, hard midday

light, in the opalescence of late afternoon or in the crisp brilliance of a winter evening when the glitter-ing lights add a beauty of their own to the scene before us of towering buildings and sleek ferryboats.

Soon after the fort was torn down, another building went up at the tip of Manhattan: one with circular walls familiar to the millions who remember the old Aquarium in Battery Park. Built originally as a fort during the War of 1812, Castle Clinton stood on a pile of rocks south of the mainland. In 1824 it was converted into an amusement place, the famed Castle Garden, and a long covered bridge joined it to Battery Park. Next it became the Immigrant Station (1855) and in 1896 was opened as the Aquarium. Now the circle is complete, for only the original fort walls of Castle Clinton remain.

J. Clarence Davies Collection, Museum of the City of New York

Museum of the City of New York

Since the 1790's there has been a tree-shaded Battery promenade offering a magnificent harbor view. The original walk was along State Street and the park land was added little by little until 1870. Since the completion of the Brooklyn-Battery tunnel, the park has come into its own again, and this patch of green, though dwarfed by the skyscrapers, still boasts its tree-lined promenade, fort and view.

RECISTRING EMIGRANTS

By 1890 more than seven and a half million new-comers from all corners of the world, seeking a new life in a new land, poured into America through Castle Garden, the portal of New York.

Many of them settled right here in the city and formed a large part of New York's tremendously increasing population which totaled 312,000 in 1840; 515,000 in 1850; and 814,000 in 1860.

From the original negative by Jacob A. Riis, Museum of the City of New York

In 1855 when Castle Garden became the Immigrant Station, the Irish and the Germans were the nationalities which arrived in the greatest numbers. Later in the century more and more people came from other countries, especially from Italy, Poland, Russia, Greece and Hungary.

Packed into unbelievably crowded quarters on immigrant ships, these bewildered foreigners landed in this strange new place wearing the dress of their homelands, knowing only the customs of the countries they had left behind. Castle Garden was the confusing, noisy center where they were met by relatives and friends, by agents, sometimes by swindlers. From here they set out to make their way in the new world. All too often the gateway to liberty led to what seemed to be a deadend—the sweatshop. Lack of English and ignorance of American ways made this the only available place to work.

They settled, whenever possible, near people from home, seeking the comfort of their own kind. Soon New York had dozens of small foreign sections where neighbors spoke the language of the old country.

These foreign sections remain firmly entrenched today, although the second and third generations, born and brought up here, are New Yorkers all. Yorkville, once a separate village, has for years been the large German center. In this area around Third Avenue and 86th Street you will find delicatessen stores full of sausages and marzipan; German bakeries and beer stubes with costumed waiters.

The great Jewish section is in the lower east side where Manhattan bulges out into the East River and Delancey Street bisects the district from the Bowery to the river. The demand for yarmilkes and Torah mantles started many a shopkeeper in business in the 1880's and 1890's. Today another generation carries the same stock—plus the flag and many of the products of the new Republic of Israel.

New York is dotted with "Little Italys" from Bleecker Street on the west side, to Mulberry Street on the east, and to East Harlem uptown.

Mott, Pell and Doyer Streets, just west of the Bowery at Chatham Square, mark Chinatown's center.

Much of the old Syrian quarter along Washington and Greenwich Streets was wiped out with the construction of the Brooklyn-Battery tunnel.

Many of the Greeks located in the Chelsea area, around Eighth Avenue in the West Twenties.

Harlem, that wide area stretching from Central Park to the Harlem River, from Morningside Avenue to the East River, is home to many thousands of Negroes, Italians and Puerto Ricans. Formally founded in 1658, Harlem flourished for over two hundred years as a separate community. With the building of the Elevated in the 1870's the section was soon engulfed by the expanding city. After 1900 the Negroes, attracted by low rentals, began to move in, and within twenty years, with the influx of World War I workers, Harlem was entirely Negro. The section southeast had already become a "Little Italy," crowded with emigrants from southern Italy.

Three friends resting after a day of play on a Harlem street.

Latest to develop was Spanish Harlem, the district east of Central Park between 96th and 125th Streets. This was one of the first parts of New York to become a center for Puerto Ricans. Coming as they did with very little money, they could afford only the cheapest living quarters. Since then they have spread out to many other sections of Manhattan such as upper Broadway, the region west of Central Park and the Chelsea area in the West Twenties. In these localities movie houses show Spanish pictures, the *bodega* and the *lavendaria automatica* replace the grocery and laundrymat, and restaurants feature Spanish cooking. By 1954 there were 450,000 Puerto Ricans here, nearly double the number of 1950. Again there is a repetition of the century-old situation, as lack of training and ignorance of the language make only the lowest jobs available.

About 250,000 other newcomers, mostly Europeans, also settled in the city during the years 1946 to 1952.

Broadway, the oldest street on Manhattan Island, is an appropriate starting point for an exploration of new and old New York. Back in the Dutch days you could look from the fort right up Broadway as far as the gate in the wall at the north end of town. The open space in front of the fort was used from time to time as a market place or as a parade ground. In 1733 it was first leased as a bowling green and thus becomes New York's oldest existing park. Just before the Revolution it was fenced in and the statue of George III erected—only to be torn down by wrathful Americans in 1776. During that same year Washington had his headquarters in the house at the extreme left, the famous Kennedy mansion at 1 Broadway. This house remained standing for years; the drawing below shows it in 1830. Because of the many handsome homes there, lower Broadway remained a residential section for a long time. Between the trees you can catch a glimpse of the slender spire of Trinity Church while, on the right, with the cupola, stands the large Adelphi Hotel. Most important to the residents then were the gas street lamps, a recent civic improvement, infinitely superior to the old oil lamps. No Croton water yet, hence the pump by the Green; and only very rough paving blocks for the horseback riders and carriage passengers to joggle over.

Today at Bowling Green only the park itself has resisted the encroachment of business. The Washington Building (1 Broadway) and the curved façade of the Standard Oil Building (26 Broadway) tower overhead. Electric lights or the more recent mercury vapor street lights and smooth asphalt, however, offer more comfort than the gas lamps and paving stones of the 1830's.

Looking along Rector Street, toward Broadway and 1 Wall Street (the Irving Trust Building).

The long horizontal New York of the 1850's has become the towering vertical city of the 1950's. The first step was the elevator which made many-storied structures possible. It had passed the experimental stage and was ready to begin a practical business career when the Equitable Life Assurance Society in 1870 installed elevators in its new office building at 120 Broadway. Then in the mid-seventies the march upward started with the Western Union Building, 230 feet, and the Tribune Tower, 260 feet. At this point brick walls and cast iron façades bowed to a new principle of construction, a steel skeleton which supported the walls and floors of the building. Now you could get height without thickness of walls. The first of this type to be erected in New York was the Tower Building at 50 Broadway, put up in 1888–89. From then on the advance was rapid until we reached such great heights as the Singer Building, 149 Broadway, 612 feet (1907), and the Woolworth Building, 233 Broadway, 792 feet (1913). New York streets were disappearing in the shadows below. To try and retain light and air for the man in the street, in 1916 Zoning Laws were instituted which regulated the height of buildings by setbacks (their height in relation to the width of the street) and by the percentage of the lot which was to be covered at specified heights. This was the start of the terrace and tower design. Today on lower Manhattan the highest buildings are the 60 Wall Tower at 70 Pine Street, 950 feet; the Bank of Manhattan, 40 Wall Street, 927 feet; the City Bank, Farmers Trust at 20 Exchange Place, 741 feet; and the Irving Trust (*shown here*), 1 Wall Street, 654 feet.

J. Clarence Davies Collection, Museum of the City of New York

The twenty years between the 1830's and the 1850's transformed lower Broadway from a pleasant residential quarter into a crowded, noisy business street. Houses were converted into stores or were replaced by narrow four- and five-story office buildings with severely plain, monotonous façades.

Wall Street has played many roles. To the Dutch it meant the northern boundary of the original settlement and, after 1653, a sturdy wall built for protection against Indians. To the English colony it was a street topped by Trinity Church, lined with handsome Georgian homes and the site of the City Hall (erected in 1704 at the corner of Nassau Street). To Americans after the Revolution it meant the seat of national government, with President Washington's offices in Federal Hall. Then came the rapid transition to business: merchants' offices, stores and banks, until by 1850 Wall Street meant a great financial center. By 1916 the street had assumed the familiar appearance in the photograph at the right.

Wall Street, 1821, a street of churches, stores, remodeled houses and the second Trinity Church.

Museum of the City of New York

Wall Street, 1850, a street of merchants' offices, banks and the present Trinity Church.

J. Clarence Davies Collection, Museum of the City of New York

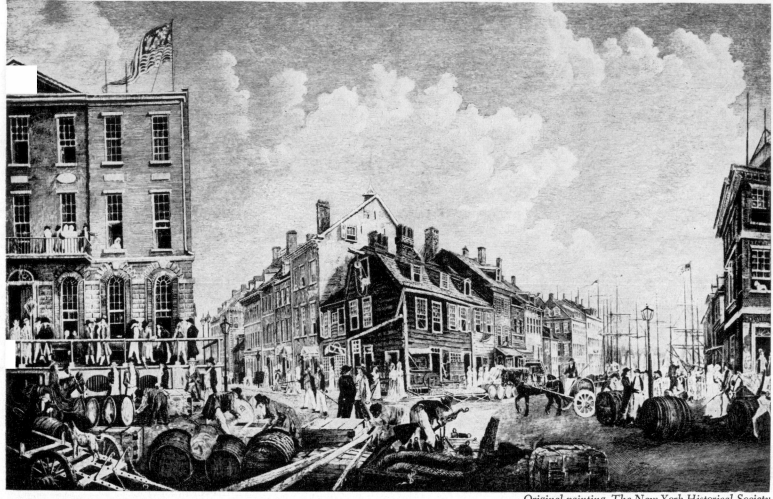

Corner of Wall and Water Streets, 1800.

Tontine Coffee House at left, Merchants' at right.

Coffee House Slip was the old name for the lower end of Wall Street because here were the popular coffee houses: the Merchants', the Tontine, the Exchange and the Phoenix—handy meeting places for the merchants whose ships docked nearby. Much business was carried on in the coffee houses as the merchants negotiated for imports from Europe and the Far East, and arranged for further distribution of American goods. Conveniently near, too, were their warehouses where they did a flourishing wholesale and retail business. Today at this same corner of Wall and Water Streets coffee still dominates, but for another reason. This is the center of the coffee trade and the smell of coffee covers the neighborhood on a damp day. Trinity Church still stands at the head of Wall Street. The 1699 building burned in 1776; the second, erected after the Revolution, was demolished in 1839; and in 1846 the present church was dedicated—a church as famous as the street itself.

By 1740 the New York-Brooklyn ferry was well established, with two rowboats for passengers, two scows, or periguas, for cattle and a brick ferry house on the Brooklyn side (Fulton Street).

Crossing to Brooklyn in 1840 (the Fulton Street ferry), you rode on boats with the familiar skimming-dish shape and heard the familiar creaking of piles as the ferry eased into the curved arms of the slip.

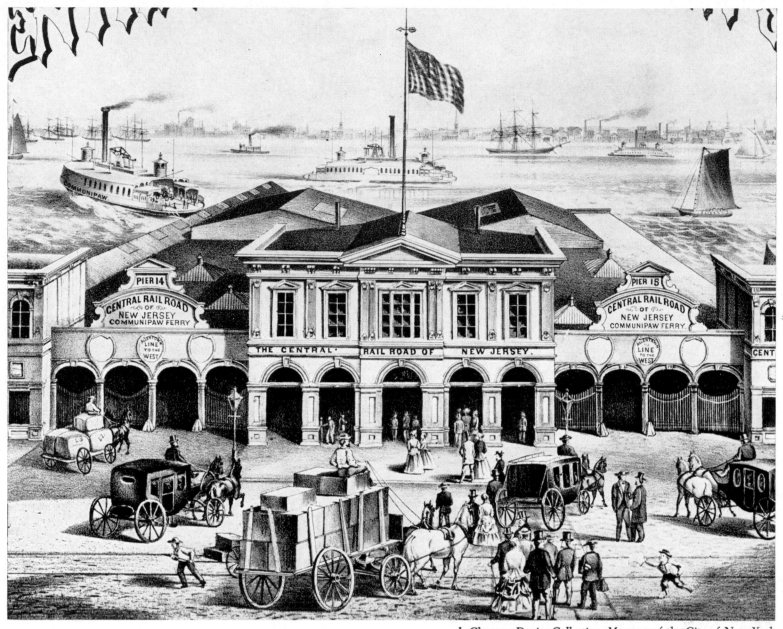

The ferry boat to New Jersey . . . to Staten Island
. . . to Brooklyn. It was the only way to get there, and
service was intermittent at first. Even after there was
a schedule, the sailboat combating tide and head
winds might take three hours to cross the Hudson.
Robert Fulton, fresh from triumphs with the "Cler-
mont," in 1812 designed a steam ferry, a vessel of
very different shape—two separate hulls, decked over,
with a wheel between, and the steam engine in the
center. The boat was the same fore and aft with a
rudder at each end so it could go either way. By the
time the above picture was drawn in 1867 ferries were
at their peak. People arriving from the south or west
had to take the ferry from the railroad terminals on
the Jersey shore. Commuters in increasing numbers
were making the daily trip to lower Manhattan. On
the East River alone a dozen lines connected New
York with neighboring Brooklyn.

No more ferries on the East
River, but thousands of passengers
still cross the Hudson every day.

During the 1930's sixty million ferry passengers used to cross the Hudson annually. Now a steadily increasing majority come via the Lincoln and Holland tunnels and over the George Washington Bridge. Each year finds fewer ferry boats on the river. However, from the ferry you get a good view of the ships (ten thousand a year enter the New York-New Jersey waterfront area) and if you're lucky you may see a transatlantic liner steaming along with her attendant tugs or maybe even a welcome on a maiden voyage.

The Staten Island ferry comes in with full loads just as it has for years—no alternate means of transportation for the commuters making the five-mile trip across the bay. New York's visitors swell the throng, for the view from the ferry is a "must" on every sight-seer's list. These streamlined three-deckers are a far cry from the tiny flat-bottomed perigua with which the sixteen-year-old Cornelius Vanderbilt began his ferry service back in 1810. Most of the streaming crowds help swell the throngs at nearby subways.

Dutch houses were still standing in 1831 when this view of Broad Street looking toward Wall was drawn before the great fire.

Red brick and brownstone lined Broad Street during the 1880's when this photograph was taken from Wall Street looking South.

The last of Dutch New York disappeared in the Great Fire of 1835, which spread through the Broad Street, Wall Street and East River area wiping out 700 buildings. This section was immediately rebuilt and business forged ahead swiftly. The New York Stock Exchange, which had been organized in 1792, established itself at 10-12 Broad Street in 1865 (*building at extreme right*). This was demolished in 1901 and the present Stock Exchange erected on the same site. The New York Curb Exchange met outdoors on Broad Street for years. In 1921 it moved into a building on Trinity Place and in 1953 became the American Stock Exchange.

Photograph of Curb Exchange (*opposite*) business being conducted in the street about 1903.

Leonard Hassam Bogart Collection, Museum of the City of New York

A Dutchman's desire for a canal in New Amsterdam accounts for Broad Street's unusual width.

Pine Street is a gash carved by a giant in the steel and concrete mass that is lower Manhattan today.

The famous New Dutch Church, built in 1731 and demolished in 1882, played various roles during its long life. It was in turn a church, a prison and a riding school for the British, a church again and then a post office.

The church has another claim to fame because this picture is the earliest street view we have of the city. During New York's first hundred years the various artists had concentrated on bird's-eye views and panoramas. Just after the New Dutch Church was completed in 1731 this charming picture was made of the corner of Nassau and Liberty (then Crown) Streets. Stilted though it is, the artist captured the flavor of the colonial town by the care with which he reproduced the details around him. Weathercocks and cobblestones, fence and turnstile, horseback rider and pedestrians. The lone coach heading toward Liberty Street was one of the first in the city and gave no hint of traffic problems to come. A sad commentary, indeed, is the photograph of the same corner today, with the dark tall buildings blocking out the sky, and one-way traffic filling the alley-like street.

There was more religious tolerance here than in other colonies, and by 1776 New York's churches included Baptist, Episcopal, Lutheran, Methodist, Moravian, Presbyterian and Reformed Dutch (the denomination of the original settlers). There were Hebrew synagogues and Friends' meeting houses. The first Roman Catholic church was erected in 1786.

J. Clarence Davies Collection, Museum of the City of New York

A nostalgic view of John Street in 1768, painted years later, recalls city life in the pre-Revolutionary War days. An historical spot, too, for just a block east was Golden Hill where the first blood of the Revolution was shed on January 19, 1770, in a short but lively skirmish known as the Battle of Golden Hill. It was a residential section of small modest wooden homes, their steep roofs reminiscent of the early Dutch houses. This south side of John Street between William and Nassau was dominated by the Methodist Episcopal Church which had just been put up. Ever since then there has been a Methodist church on this site, but today's building is dwarfed by the offices that surround it. Dark and dirty, the modern street is a noisy, narrow clutter of trucks and cars. Instead of a hitching post, at the curb is a parking meter.

How to get quick, cheap transportation for New York's increasing population? Perhaps build a pneumatic tube and drive the cars by compressed air? Or run the cars by cables which are driven by stationary engines installed at half-mile intervals along the tracks? Charles Harvey tried this, as shown at left. But it was impractical. Steam engines proved to be the answer, and under a Rapid Transit Board two companies built tracks and had four miles in operation by 1874. Ten years later four El lines ran all the way to the Harlem River.

Harvey's elevated railroad on Greenwich Street, demonstrated in 1868.

J. Clarence Davies Collection, Museum of the City of New York

Steam engines pulling the elevated trains along the Bowery in 1895.

J. Clarence Davies Collection, Museum of the City of New York

The El became a mixed blessing as the years rolled by: it was slum-producing, noisy and a hindrance to traffic. Its death knell was sounded in the 1930's and nearly all the lines are now gone. This pattern of shadows on Division Street is only a memory. Soon all rapid transit in New York will be underground.

There was adventure in an El ride. Remember the curves at 110th Street and 8th Avenue, at 53rd Street where you swung in from 6th or 9th Avenue? And this one at Coenties Slip near South Ferry where the old El framed the modern International Telephone and Telegraph Building?

When you climbed the steps to the El you entered a different world. First there was the Swiss chalet-like station with its pot-bellied stove and colored glass windows. There was the ticket chopper who "chopped" the green ticket that you dropped in his box. Then there was the world you saw from the El windows: the intimate glimpses of life in a dingy cold-water flat; the Bowery flop-houses; and people at work in a dimly lit loft. When the El reached downtown it glided along between tall buildings, mysterious and dark, with barely enough room for the tracks to squeeze between the two rows of houses. If you were alert you could catch a quick glimpse of a sliver of city street—Cedar, Pine or Wall. By 1954 only one short section of the Third Avenue line was left.

The Elevated, extending south from 20th Street, stretched like a silver highway down the length of Ninth Avenue.

Yesterday's solution became today's problem and the Elevated bowed to motor traffic's need for open avenues. This is the same location in 1947.

Photograph by Byron, Museum of the City of New York

Photograph by Byron, Museum of the City of New York

In front of the Casino Theater, Broadway and 39th Street, in 1896.

Motor traffic began, of course, with the horseless carriage. Here are two city models, a converted brougham and a hansom cab in 1896, with a blue-coated traffic cop right at hand. By 1900 cars had so advanced that New York could have its first automobile show. Most people were getting their enjoyment from a ride on the open trolley, the summer model of the new streetcar. It was quite a job at that to clamber up the high step along the side and squeeze in on a crowded cross seat.

End of line, Broadway and 23rd Street, 1901.

Photograph by Byron, The Byron Collection, Museum of the City of New York

Automobiles lined up on Broadway
from 59th to 60th Streets, 1918.

High up on wheels whether you were in a touring-car, racing-car or truck. This was 1918 and, as a war time measure, drivers were demonstrating how to meet the gasoline shortage by using kerosene. The motor age had arrived. In 1907 the Fifth Avenue buses had switched from horses to motors, and in 1917 the last horsecar wound its way along West Street. The electric trolley was at the height of its popularity, having been introduced in 1888. (Now it, too, has disappeared completely from the streets of Manhattan and buses have taken over all surface transportation.) New Yorkers went underground in 1904 when the first subway was opened from City Hall to West 145th Street. By 1908 the subway was linking Manhattan, the Bronx and Brooklyn, and a decade later the "shuttle" between Times Square and Grand Central introduced a new struggle as people tried to "follow the green line." The B.M.T. and the Independent (Eighth Avenue) lines completed the modern system.

Broadway, looking north from
Cortlandt Street, about 1880.

Perhaps the most distinguishing feature of New York streets in the
seventies and eighties was the mass of telephone and telegraph wires
overhead. Telegraph wires began to go up in 1845 and telephone wires
in 1877. By the 1880's the situation was so bad that the city fathers
ordered all wires placed underground, and the blizzard of '88, by dam-
aging many wires, furthered this work enormously. However, yesterday's roofs crisscrossed with wires are matched today by an equally distinctive sight—the jumble of television aerials that cover the housetops.
For all the physical changes that seventy years have brought to Broadway, the same feeling prevails in both these views. Traffic is equally confusing whether it be horse-drawn buses, delivery wagons and victorias, or
gasoline-driven buses, trailer-trucks and streamlined taxis. One building
remains the same, the old Sun Building at the northeast corner of Broadway and Chambers Street. Plainly seen jutting into Broadway in the
early view, it is seen halfway up the street in the modern photograph.

Broadway, looking north from
1 Broadway, today.

J. Clarence Davies Collection, Museum of the City of New York

The oldest building standing on Broadway, in fact the oldest church on Manhattan, is St. Paul's Chapel, part of Trinity Parish. Built in 1766 and completed in 1793 with the addition of a steeple, the church has changed amazingly little in appearance during 160 years. In 1798, when the above drawing was made, St. Paul's drew its congregation from the nearby homes, for Broadway and Fulton Street were still lined with small comfortable brick houses, gambrel-roofed and dormer-windowed. It was a residential section with activity centering around the corner street pump. (The following year the Manhattan Company was incorporated to supply the city of 60,000 with water. Six miles of wooden pipes were laid, but though this system was later extended, the supply was never adequate.) St. Paul's has particular historical significance because George Washington, on the day in 1789 that he was inaugurated, led a procession from Federal Hall in Wall Street to the church for a special service. He continued to worship at St. Paul's during the sixteen months he was in the city.

J. Clarence Davies Collection, Museum of the City of New York

Fifty years later quiet residential Broadway hummed with business activity. St. Paul's portico, still plainly seen, is now flanked by stores and the fashionable Astor House. Further down the street looms the spire of Trinity Church, the recently completed third building to stand on that site. Eye-catching posters advertise P. T. Barnum's Museum, mecca for both visitors and New Yorkers. The museum was to go up in smoke in 1865 in a fire spectacular enough to suit even Barnum himself. Looking down Broadway from this same point today, St. Paul's holds its own but Trinity barely shows. The angular corner of Barnum's is repeated in the present office building at Broadway and Ann Street. Although the number of pedestrians is similar, today's people lose their importance in this street of tall buildings. As for St. Paul's itself, Sunday worshippers now come from afar, but during the busy week days neighborhood office workers find both church and the quiet old graveyard restful spots for any spare minutes.

The Bakewell View (1717–1746) of the Great Dock along the East River.

The Birch View of New York City from Brooklyn Heights, 1802.

The city and the sea make a vital chapter in New York's history. As early as 1676 it was necessary to build the Great Dock (*upper left picture*) to take care of the many small sloops and river boats that plied the local waters. Then came the need for slips and wharves where the larger ships could tie up, particularly along the East River. By 1802 if you looked at the city from Brooklyn Heights (*upper right picture*), the entire shore was edged with masts. Forty years later New York was the busiest port in the country. Clippers loaded their cargoes for the Far East, and steam packets were readied for the passengers that they took on scheduled crossings to Europe. Schooners for the coastal trade were tied up next to barges from the Erie Canal, while the newer steamers were landing at recently completed wharves along the Hudson. When the photograph below was taken from the tower of Brooklyn Bridge in 1876, tall masts still dominated the waterfront, but steamers had assumed the leading role in shipping.

South Street's lofty masts have given way to squat funnels and angular cranes, and yesterday's open wharves to large covered piers. However, to many New Yorkers today the port means nothing. To them the East River is only a longer distance between subway stops, on their way to the office.

Looking down from Brooklyn Bridge today there is still one reminder of the past. The old slant-roofed houses that dominated the 1876 view cling to the filled-in area along the waterfront while modern Manhattan towers above them, its foundation securely resting on the bedrock of the island.

In 1828 South Street and Maiden Lane teemed with shipping activity; business was transacted in the open; drays and wagons, barrels and bales cluttered streets and wharves. In 1953 at the same corner trucks thundered by, but business had vanished indoors. Today even the street itself has disappeared from view—covered by the new South Street viaduct.

South Street was the very center of things in those boom days of the nineteenth century. As all sailing ships docked there, the merchants established offices in the nearby houses, and so kept an actual eye on the loading and unloading, inspected cargoes, and saw to it that the ships were properly outfitted. Crowded in among the merchants' offices and the shipping lines were the shops of sailmakers, coopers and ship chandlers, filled with the thousand and one things needed for a year-long voyage. The merchants were the backbone of New York's commerce, and they were turning the city into a huge distribution center. In 1825 the Erie Canal had been opened. Now barges brought goods from upstate and the western territory right into New York. Merchants then shipped these goods on to other Atlantic coast cities or to Europe. Meanwhile clipper ships were bringing in cargoes from the east and these also passed through the merchants' hands and went on out to the rest of the country. This business became so big that during the 1840's over two-thirds of the imports of the entire nation were entering through New York Harbor. Some of the ships themselves came from local yards. In 1827 the ships built here included: 3 brigs, 23 ships, 49 schooners, 68 sloops, 12 steamboats, 15 tow boats and 19 canal boats. In the 1840's and 50's these yards produced some of the fastest clipper ships in the world and they established new records for their merchant owners.

For more than a hundred and thirty years there has been a market at the corner of South and Fulton Streets. Originally a general retail market where local householders bought their daily meat, vegetables and other foods, it gradually changed until now it is the largest wholesale fish market along the Atlantic seaboard—500,000 to 1,000,000 pounds of fish are brought in daily either directly by fishing boats or in large trucks from New England ports. Modern refrigeration and deepfreeze methods have also banished the old-time fish-cars or floating crates that, tied to the wharves, held the day's catch in the river waters.

Museum of the City of New York

Fulton Fish Market by moonlight, about 1876.

Fulton Fish Market at sunrise, 1950, during the peak of business.

In spite of the increasing number of trucks, there are still many fishing boats tying up at the Fulton Market pier. Fishing boats are the only commercial vessels entering New York still equipped with sails.

North of Fulton Street rise the piers of Brooklyn Bridge. The massive granite towers, the contrasting delicacy of the cables and the grace of the span present one of the most beautiful sights in the city. The building of the bridge took a great toll: the life of the designer, John A. Roebling, permanent injury to his son, Washington A. Roebling, who carried through the task, and the lives of a score of workmen. Construction began in 1870 and the bridge was opened May 27, 1883, with a gigantic fireworks celebration and a huge crowd, for everybody turned out to see this first bridge connecting New York and the neighboring city of Brooklyn. Truly, a world's wonder.

The New-York Historical Society

Building the Brooklyn Bridge: from the Brooklyn shore, March, 1877.

Floating derrick, New York Harbor, 1869.

Cranes have always been vital to waterfront activity, be it shipbuilding or the loading of cargoes. The earliest views of New Amsterdam show a simple but sturdy crane handy to the first wharf, while this floating derrick used in 1869 was considered very efficient in the nineteenth century. Today all kinds of loading equipment have been developed: fork-lift trucks and mobile cranes, straddle-lift carriers and heavy cranes. These two great cranes express to an extraordinary degree their latent power as they rise above the Brooklyn Navy Yard.

Heavy crane, Brooklyn Navy Yard, today.

Two hundred and fifty tons can be lifted by one of these heavy cranes which effortlessly swing a locomotive through the air. These are the behemoths of the waterfront, the most powerful machines used in the harbor. Not only do they handle approximately 150,000,000 short tons of freight annually, but they do an enormous amount of salvage work with stranded or sunken vessels.

Back to the heart of the city, to the City Hall on the park, that triangular plot between Broadway and Park Row. This was a gracious setting for the new City Hall, with handsome town houses, rows of shade trees and St. Paul's Chapel at the far left. The artist of 1819 faithfully included the famous jarring note—New York's pigs.

When Joseph Mangin and John McComb designed City Hall they gave us one of our finest buildings. They created an interior with a beautiful double-curved staircase, and with rooms decorated with delicate carving. The building was completed with a cupola topped with a figure of justice (the cross in the 1819 view is the artist's error).

City Hall remains in its original beauty, and passers-by still enjoy the tree-shaded spot as much as they did in 1819. In 1953 special celebrations here marked the 300th anniversary of municipal government. In 1653 the responsibility for local affairs was given to the citizens and they established the original City Hall on Pearl Street. In 1704 the second City Hall was built at Wall and Nassau, and in 1812 this third building was completed. Nearly 150 years in the same spot—quite a record for this constantly changing city.

View of Murray Street from Broadway to Church Street, north side, 1855.

Nearby is Murray Street which extends from City Hall Park westward to the Hudson River. The wave of commercialism that was sweeping the city to new heights of prosperity affected this region, and by 1855, Murray Street had been transformed into an up-to-date business center. Aside from the fairly large Manhattan Hotel, the street was crammed with stores selling boots and shoes, clothing, hats and even the new-fangled sewing machine. No wonder that Columbia College, a block away, was about to leave this commercial setting for the country-like region around Madison Avenue and 49th Street. The quantities of boxes and bales that cluttered the sidewalks and the number of carts and wagons passing by were appalling. However, this can be matched in Murray Street today, for you walk along a pavement piled with cartons and blocked with men who are loading trucks. Strangely enough, many of the old houses look down on you, for this locality is a mixture of old and new.

View of Park Row, looking
northeast from Broadway, 1830.

Going back to the days when City Hall Park had
charm and elegance, another view which captured these
qualities shows Park Row and the eastern edge of the
park in 1830. The large building with arched windows
and doors is the well-known Park Theater. The spire of
Brick Presbyterian Church rises above the roof tops, and
City Hall is hidden in the trees at the left. The street
has gone commercial, however, and many old houses
have been converted into shops. In spite of this, the
1830 bow windows give the shops an attractive air that
is sadly lacking in the 1855 Murray Street on the opposite page. The same corner today is distinctly reminiscent because the basic city patterns of pedestrians, traffic and streets remain unchanged although the line of
coaches is replaced by a string of buses, cobblestones by
asphalt and gas lamps by electricity. Structures, on the
other hand, come and go. Planned for early demolition
is the domed World Building, once the city's highest.

Museum of the City of New York

On March 12-14, 1888, 20.9 inches of snow. Group on New Street, looking toward Wall.

"A great white hurricane roared all day through New York yesterday and turned the comfortable city into a wild and bewildering waste of snow and ice. . . . When day broke the city presented an amazing appearance. . . . At every turn could be seen these deserted vehicles." *New York Herald,* March 13, 1888.

There never *was* such a storm as the Blizzard of '88, according to everyone who saw it. Perhaps the surprise of snow so late in the season had something to do with it. At any rate, it completely disrupted city transportation; households ran out of food and fuel; and communication lines were down all over the place. Although telephone and telegraph wires are intact in this picture, so much damage was done in other streets that the plan to put all wires underground moved rapidly forward and the familiar poles and cross-arms soon disappeared from New York's streets. Fortunately for the present generation who had missed the '88 blizzard, on December 26, 1947, another great storm arrived, one that broke all records. Once again there was a "wild and bewildering waste of snow," once again "deserted vehicles" filled the street. Once again a storm paralyzed the busy city as nature emphasized her strength and her superiority.

On December 26-27, 1947, 25.8 inches of snow. West 22nd Street, looking toward Eighth Avenue.

It is hard to realize that a blizzard could have any effect on this wall of steel and concrete. Even the familiar island of Manhattan has ceased to exist and the buildings appear to rise from the very bones of the earth. Again it seems as though giants have taken over and made a savage metropolis out of what was once a primitive settlement. And primitive it was. The first shelters were, the report read, "hovels and holes" and houses "built of the bark of trees." These quickly gave way to wooden houses with thatched roofs. By 1650 brick and stone, slate and tile were proving their worth as durable, fire-resistant material. Incredible as it seems, the two pictures on these pages have been reproduced in the same scale. Both show the edge of the Hudson River which is the sole point of similarity in this contrast of 1650 and 1950.

New Amsterdam in 1651, 120 houses and 1,000 inhabitants.

Downtown Manhattan seen from the Lehigh Valley Railroad
Terminal Slip on the New Jersey side of the Hudson River.

The Hudson River waterfront developed later than the East River, growing up with the nineteenth century. Not only sailing vessels but steamers of the various Long Island Sound and Boston lines docked here, and the stately white Hudson River side-wheelers that carried passengers to the lands on upper Manhattan. Here, too, were wharfs and sheds for the passengers and freight ferried across from the railroad terminals on the Jersey side.

Southern end of West Street, along the Hudson, 1860's.

The development of modern West Street began with the long row of uniform piers, built on the recommendation of the New York City Improvement Commission in 1907. Today the activity in this most valuable section of New York's waterfront is three-fold. Ships dock here with passengers and freight; railroads terminating in New Jersey still use nearly as many piers as the steamship lines; while the railroad tracks of the New York Central bring in great carloads of goods both for distribution and transshipment. Quantities of foodstuff come through here, especially dairy products, fruits and vegetables for local consumers.

The needs of a mechanized city also changed West Street. At the lower end is the Brooklyn-Battery tunnel, opened in 1950. Over 16,000,000 cars use this tunnel annually.

Cars moving, cars standing still—equal traffic problems. Here one solution solves both as West Street becomes a parking space for some while other cars speed by on the Highway overhead.

Elevated and express highways, clover-leaf intersections, over-passes and tunnels—bewildering products of the motor age that change the face of the city. Looking like an army of giant insects, cars advance in a phalanx along one of these highways. Friday evening finds lines heading both in and out of the city—in such hordes that nowhere can you now enjoy the pleasures of driving on the open road.

George Washington Bridge,
spanning the Hudson River.

Hudson River ferry at Dyckman Street, New York.

The Dyckman Street ferry, with its walking-beam, plodded back and forth across the Hudson for many years until it bowed finally to the demands of today. Only the Jeffrey's Hook lighthouse on a point near the Manhattan pier of the bridge remains to remind us of yesterday's life along the waterfront. In 1931 the great span of the George Washington Bridge was completed and New York City and New Jersey were at last connected by a bridge. It is the second longest suspension bridge in the country (the Golden Gate Bridge in San Francisco is longer) and more than 27,000,000 cars cross it yearly. The approach to the city from the lofty Palisades above Fort Lee, across the sweeping Hudson and on to the labyrinth of roads at the Manhattan end, is as breath-taking as is the view shown here of the bridge itself from the New York shore.

The pattern of steel makes the piers of the George Washington Bridge a fitting portal to modern New York.

Incredible as was the growth in the fifty years prior to 1854, that of the succeeding fifteen years was equally so. By 1869 the entire island seemed alive. Rows of houses had sprung up far north of 42nd Street and factories had put in their appearance all over central Manhattan. No wonder, for nearly 950,000 people lived and worked here now, and business had taken great strides forward since the end of the Civil War. Easily spotted is the newly laid out Central Park, an area saved just in time from the grasp of the growing city. Along the Hudson River are many more piers and larger ships, while at the tip of the island Battery Park has been filled in and Castle Garden is no longer an island.

Manhattan's present street plan was drawn up in 1807 by commissioners who suggested a gridiron plan. They backed it up with this statement: "A city is to be composed principally of the habitations of men, and straight-sided and right-angled houses are the most cheap to build, and the most convenient to live in." Hence our right-angled rows of numbered avenues and streets.

The city's population of 93,000 in 1810 had grown to more than 600,000 when this sketch of New York was drawn in 1854. By then the city extended to 42nd Street. North of that were the villages of Yorkville, Harlem and Manhattanville; a generous sprinkling of farms, taverns and country houses; the aqueducts and reservoirs of the Croton Water Company and the railroad tracks of the New York and Harlem Railroad.

J. Clarence Davies Collection, Museum of the City of New York

Here is the whole, the modern city, whose component parts we have been looking at one by one. Here they are fitted together section by section: the waterfronts with their great piers, the skyscrapers of lower Manhattan, the midtown business district, the low roofs of Harlem and the bridges that join the boroughs and link them to nearby communities.

The dark patches of Central Park and Riverside Drive, preserving what little is left of Manhattan's natural topography, stand out clearly, as do Washington Square and Tompkins Square. Just beyond the latter emerge the new patterns of the city—those made by housing developments such as Peter Cooper Village, Stuyvesant Town, Jacob Riis and Lillian Wald Houses. Units such as these are breaking up that gridiron plan set nearly a century and a half ago.

Here, too, is the summary of over three hundred years of history, the culmination of all the incidents and efforts of the past. And going back for a minute to those early days of the Dutch, imagine Peter Stuyvesant's reaction if he could have looked upon this.

Fairchild Aerial Surveys, Inc.

The road to Hellgate ferry, 86th Street and the East River, sketch by Eliza Greatorex, 1869.

The city of today was made at the sacrifice of places like this when natural topography gave way to prosaic city blocks. In the late 1860's Eliza Greatorex sought to preserve in a series of sketches the fast disappearing romantic flavor of the old New York countryside, such as this Hellgate ferry approach at East 86th Street.

Few bits remain. If you walk along this same East 86th Street today you will come to Henderson Place, a back water of small houses holding its own against the surrounding apartments, while just beyond stands the lovely Gracie Mansion, now official home of New York's mayor.

Museum of the City of New York

On Broadway there was much to catch the romantic eye of Eliza Greatorex. Typical of the old Dutch farmhouses scattered through Manhattan was this sloping-roofed Hopper family home at 50th Street. Fortunately, in the outlying districts a few of these have been preserved even to the present.

The cool shade of the thick trees around the Hopper House must have been welcomed on a summer afternoon, but today as you walk up Broadway from 50th Street it is only the "healthfully air-cooled" theater that offers relief from the hot sun.

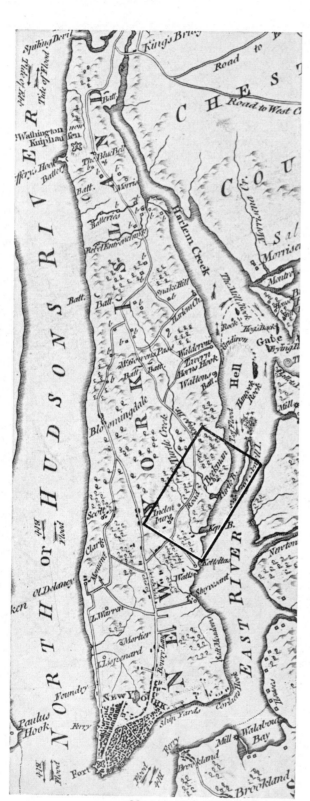

The old-time mapmaker had a simple task compared with modern demands when it comes to mapping Manhattan. Cameras, however, can produce wonders. This picture was made in 1940 for the U. S. Coast and Geodetic Survey by an Army Air Force photographer using a nine-lens camera developed for

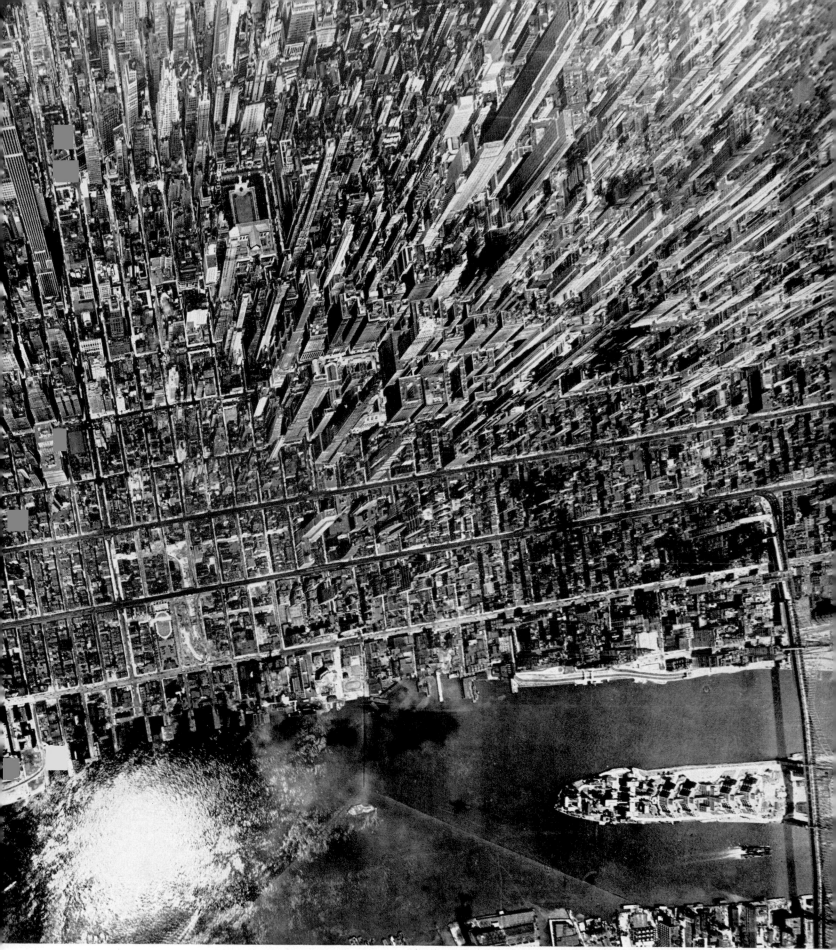

aerial mapmaking. He was focusing directly down on 34th Street and the East River, and caught the reflection of the noon sun on the water.

This mid-Manhattan section of the city has strong ties with its early history. On the 1778 map it is easy to spot the same landmarks, Welfare Island (Black-

well's it was then) and Kip's Bay at the foot of the present 34th Street. Old Jacob Kip had settled there in 1654. Then in the Revolutionary War days when Washington was withdrawing to Harlem Heights after losing the Battle of Long Island, the British at Kip's Bay nearly caught the fleeing American Army.

Look down toward that same midtown Manhattan from the Triborough Bridge and you'll see a regiment of towers standing in stark relief against the sunset sky. The Chrysler and Empire State Buildings

loom up over the other office buildings and big ho-tels, while along the East River waterfront stretch the apartment houses of the Beekman-Sutton Place neigh-borhood. In this section people live as well as work.

The great buildings of Manhattan make a fitting backdrop for the big liners coming up to dock at the nearby piers, and their strength and serenity are matched by the quiet dignity of the "Queen" slowly steaming up the Hudson. The spell is broken only when the busy tugs take over the job of docking. The welcome at the time of the "Queen Mary's" maiden voyage on June 1, 1936, included all the display that the twentieth century had to offer: airplanes circling overhead, fireboats saluting with powerful streams of water and masses of small harbor craft tagging alongside the new 81,237-ton ship, the largest in the world.

Preceding two pages. The west side of midtown Manhattan, seen across the Hudson River, from Weehawken, N. J.

Crowds had packed the Battery, too, in April, 1838, to catch a glimpse of the "Great Western," 1,340 tons and 236 feet long. The city had been in a frenzy all that week, waiting to see which ship would get here first, the "Sirius" or the "Great Western." Never before had steam alone been used for a trans-Atlantic crossing and now here were two ships trying for the all-steam record. Back in 1819 the "Savannah," built in a New York ship yard, had made the first crossing under a combination of steam and sail. On April 22, the "Sirius" came in, to receive a rousing welcome—but there were plenty of cheers the next day for the "Great Western" which, although she arrived second, made the trip in fifteen and a half days, three less than had her rival. In spite of the expanse of sails shown here, they were never used in the crossing. Exactly one hundred years later, in 1938, the "Queen Mary" made her best run: 3 days, 20 hours and 42 minutes. The present record of 3 days, 10 hours and 40 minutes was made by the "United States" in 1952.

Arrival of the "Great West-
," April 23, 1838.

This section along the Hudson is best known to the ocean traveler because the big passenger liners come in here. When the "Queen Mary" arrives, she docks at one of the long 1,200-foot piers located north of 46th Street. It's a homely district of warehouses, railroad tracks and elevated highway, but a century ago it was a quiet rural locality. Country houses still occupied pleasant sites with commanding views, and fields sloped gently to the water's edge where every now and then a small rickety dock thrust itself out into the stream. Chief landmark of this region was the Latting Observatory standing near 43rd Street and Sixth Avenue. There was, however, a hint of things to come. Several factories had been established near the shore, their tall chimneys rising high on the landscape. Even more important, New York's gridiron plan of streets was beginning to press its pattern on this section of the West Forties and Fifties. Estates and farms were being divided into building lots. Hills and rocks were leveled down as new streets opened. Wooden farmhouses would soon be replaced by rows of brownstones which in turn would find themselves later giving way to apartment houses. On a few Manhattan blocks you can see all three varieties still standing together. As for the streets themselves, New York's total now is about 6,000 miles.

The New-York Historical Society

Today's highly organized waterfront north of 42nd Street, with its piers and cranes, its tugs and carfloats, is as typical of the city as are the tall buildings of Rockefeller Center in the background—an impressive contrast to the simplicity of yesterday's shore front when the Latting tower stood alone on the horizon.

The simplicity of life in 1849 is apparent in this view of New York looking south from 14th Street. There's serenity, too, in this city with its tree-lined streets, its blocks of houses and many churches. The only real activity seemed to be along the waterfront where the ships made a solid ring around the lower portion of the island. Fashionable life now centered on Union Square, having shifted north from Washington Square with its distinctive red brick, marble-trimmed houses of the 1830's. (That beautiful Square, filled with trees, is seen on the right.) Now the newly designed brownstone with its high front stoop was much sought after. Union Square itself was lovely, too, with the fountain installed a few years earlier when the city for the first time had an adequate water supply; bathrooms were now possible and brought another note of comfort to homes enjoying gaslight and stoves.

Simplicity and serenity have given way to complexity and confusion; you can fairly hear the noise of the busy city and feel its rushing pace. Home life has been replaced by business in this part of town. Masses of small manufacturing concerns and wholesale houses occupy the dingy commercial buildings and lofts that fill the side streets; clothing stores hold sway over Union Square. Washington Square, hidden in this view by hotels and apartments, is still an oasis but is rapidly losing its remaining houses and with them its atmosphere of another day. The once tree-lined streets are now hedged with parked cars. Yet it is the streets themselves that have the closest ties with the past. The Bowery continued north as Fourth Avenue and was the main road out from the city on the east side. Broadway, merging with Fourth Avenue at Union Square, forked off farther up town to become Bloomingdale Road on the western side of the island.

Washington Square on a spring day, with all the neighborhood enjoying the outdoors.

One of the many second-hand book stores on lower Fourth Avenue.

Leisure to sun, leisure to browse, leisure to look—there's still relaxation in Washington Square. The spring sun brings out the householders from Greenwich Village and the students from New York University who fill the benches under the newly budding trees while the children dig in the sand pit. The Square has a long history: potter's field, parade ground, park. Back in 1831 the newspapers announced: "Preparations are commenced for a line of superb edifices, to front on the north side of Washington Square and extending nearly the whole length of that beautiful enclosure." Those were the red brick houses which have graced the Square ever since and are now slowly disappearing to the regret of New Yorkers.

Sometimes it takes years for a new custom to strike root here, but the Washington Square outdoor art exhibit has been a success ever since its start in 1931. Twice a year, spring and fall, you can wander along and study the pictures displayed by local artists on fences and buildings of the western half of the Square. If your preference runs to books, spend those leisure moments on lower Fourth Avenue between Astor Place and 14th Street where the second-hand book dealers welcome browsers. Or if you want to stroll about, if you want variety, take a look at Fifth Avenue, starting at Washington Square where that world-famous street begins, and follow it north.

Corporal Thompson's Madison Cottage, refreshments for sportsmen, Fifth Avenue and 23rd Street, 1839–52.

Fifth Avenue, like many other streets, was opened in sections: first as far as 13th Street in 1824; from 13th to 21st in 1830; from 21st to 42nd in 1838 and from 42nd to 71st in 1851. As soon as the intersection at 23rd Street was completed, enterprising Corporal Thompson converted the old Mildeberger farmhouse into a popular roadhouse called Madison Cottage. This was replaced in 1853 by the wonderful tent-building of Franconi's Hippodrome where audiences of 10,000 watched pageants, chariot-races and gladiatorial contests. In 1859 the Fifth Avenue Hotel went up there, to become a center of fashionable activity for many years. When business claimed the locality, and stores appeared on Fifth Avenue, the hotel gave way in 1908 to the present office building.

Diagonally across 23rd Street the "Flatiron" building had gone up in 1902. An early skyscraper, it has a sturdy individuality and remains a well-known landmark in this changing scene.

Fifth Avenue Hotel, 1859–1908, accommodations for 800 guests, same site as Madison Cottage.

The Flatiron (Fuller) Building, 1902, Fifth Avenue and Broadway, 23rd to 22nd Streets at the corner of Madison Square.

Walk up Fifth Avenue from 43rd Street—walk down Fifth Avenue from 48th Street fifty years later. It's a completely different street. No stores on the avenue in 1905. Houses, churches, hotels and restaurants, that's what Fifth Avenue was made of. Well-dressed ladies in broughams and victorias were out driving or paying calls. Oh, yes, there were automobiles. Two—for this was the twentieth century.

Today it's people, people everywhere . . . faces hemming you in . . . somebody pushing . . . somebody getting in your way. Traffic's awful, too. Taxis and buses, private cars, more taxis, more buses. Never mind, try and cut through when you get a chance. We can save five seconds that way. Hurry! No leisure for drives and calls, and anyhow here on Fifth Avenue it's all business and shopping.

. . . and down below 34th Street on Fifth Avenue, traffic is even worse because, besides taxis and buses, there are the big trucks heading for the garment district over on Seventh Avenue. Everything's jammed

tightly together. No wonder when people see this snarl of traffic they sigh for the "good old days." Since this photo was taken, McCreery's has gone from 34th and Fifth and double-decker buses have disappeared.

The "good old days" meant quiet and leisurely living at 34th Street and Fifth Avenue. In the 1880's this was an extremely fashionable section with A. T. Stewart's marble palace (often called New York's finest home), William Astor's big square brownstone, and at the 33rd Street corner, the home of his brother, John Jacob Astor. In 1893 John Jacob Astor's home was replaced by the Hotel Waldorf and in 1897 the William Astor house at 34th Street was replaced by the Hotel Astoria. The resultant Waldorf-Astoria became New York's most famous hotel and flourished here until torn down in 1929 for the tallest building in the world. Today the Empire State Building (*right*) rises giantlike above 34th Street and Fifth Avenue.

Looking south on Fifth Avenue from 35th Street, summer, 1898.

In 1802, long before Fifth Avenue was opened, David Hosack bought twelve acres of pasture land and established his Elgin Botanic Garden where Rockefeller Center stands today. Medical students traveled out from town to study the plants used in drugs and medicines, while casual visitors came to stare at the strange shrubs and plants in the doctor's greenhouses. Some years later Dr. Hosack sold his land to the state, who in turn granted it to Columbia as its portion of state aid. In 1929 John D. Rockefeller, Jr., leased the land from Columbia for eighty-five years at an annual rental of $3,800,000. The concept of Rockefeller Center was a new one for the city. The area was treated not as separate city blocks but as a whole, with the individual buildings co-ordinated as part of one group. Today there are fifteen buildings on the twelve-and-a-half acres, and a population of 32,000 workers and 128,000 visitors.

Rockefeller Center: the RCA Building seen from the top floor of the Time and Life Building.

The name "Radio City" applies only to the western part of Rockefeller Center, for here are the towering RCA Building, the RKO office building, and Radio City Music Hall seating 6,200 people (the largest indoor theater in the world).

Rows of brownstone houses filled this section when the plans for Rockefeller Center were made. The Elevated was running and the Avenue of the Americas was still called Sixth Avenue in 1931 when this photograph was taken looking southeast from 51st Street and Sixth Avenue. Dr. Hosack's Elgin Botanic Garden had been divided into building lots and leased. Large imposing houses had been built on Fifth Avenue and rows of high-stooped brownstones had gone up along the side streets. These were "good" addresses in the 1880's and 1890's; then, as fashion moved away, trade and rooming-house keepers moved in; finally, with the 1920's came prohibition and the speakeasies. This neighborhood was soon thick with them: every block had its share of visitors knocking on basement doors and waiting hopefully in the dim areaways. These are the houses that little by little have been replaced by the ever-growing Rockefeller Center.

The façade of St. Patrick's Cathedral as seen from Rockefeller Center. (*Right*)

There's a pleasing formality to this Fifth Avenue crowd at the turn of the century, with their silk hats and their parasols, walking along a Fifth Avenue devoid of all shops. Marble palaces . . . horse-drawn buses . . . electric taxis . . . St. Patrick's Cathedral . . . the Union Club . . . and carriages ready to take you for a drive through Central Park.

It was only a step from the brownstone houses of West 51st Street to St. Patrick's Cathedral on Fifth Avenue. Twenty years a-building, it was dedicated in 1879. The Gothic spires which once dominated the landscape are today hidden by the many surrounding buildings, but the cathedral maintains its quiet dignity and its unique place in the lives of New Yorkers. All through the week, all day long, constant streams of people take time from their rush and business to enter the cathedral for a few minutes of prayer and quiet.

J. Clarence Davies Collection, Museum of the City of New York

Along the Grand Drive in Central Park, with the Arsenal, 64th Street and Fifth Avenue, in the background, 1869.

The plan for a Central Park was one of the best ideas that New York ever had, and it was executed so well that today the park remains essentially as it was when originally laid out. This location was first suggested in 1850, and the land, from 59th Street to 106th was assembled in 1855, the remainder, up to 110th Street, added later. In 1858 Frederick Law Olmsted and Calvert Vaux won the competition for the park plan, and they developed and completed by 1876 this pleasant place with winding driveways, tree-shaded paths, wisteria-trimmed arbors, rustic summerhouses, lakes and bridges. Many of these bits of old New York can still be found by those who like to wander and explore. To others the park is a place to enjoy the budding trees and soak up the sun of a warm spring day.

The heart of the park has always been the lake with its graceful iron bridge; the main approach was by the Mall, an imposing promenade with statues placed at intervals and ending in a grand staircase leading down to the terrace and the Bethesda Fountain at the side of the lake. You could hire a boat or feed the swans and ducks that came swimming by as you stood at the water's edge. One thing is certain, you'd have an equally good time whether you were in the hoopskirts and tall hats of the 1860's or in the slacks and shorts of the 1950's.

Age doesn't matter in Central Park, there's pleasure and a place for all: babies in carriages, youngsters on bicycles, oldsters playing croquet and chess. You can iceskate in winter and sail model boats in summer, or take your choice of a dozen other sports. You can listen to a band concert, visit the zoo, or admire the flowering shrubs and plants. For 840 acres (two and a half miles long, a half mile wide) have been snatched away from the city of stone and concrete, offering an honest-to-goodness breathing space and, conversely, a beautiful view for the hotel and apartment dwellers of the buildings that surround it. Here are beautiful shade trees, plenty of grass, lakes and pools, the Shakespearian Garden and the winding paths of the Ramble.

Sailing model boats on Conservatory Pond, east side of park, north of 72nd Street.

In Central Park you can see outcroppings of Manhattan's backbone—rocks that are 2,000,000,000 years old. Some show marks of the glacier that moved down over this area about 25,000 years ago. In contrast are today's buildings, towering high over the park, while, oblivious both of the age beneath them and the city noise beyond, the croquet-players stand, deep in their game on the sheep meadow.

At the time that land was being assembled for Central Park, the city was built up only to 42nd Street. You could get an excellent view of it all from the Latting Observatory near 43rd Street and Sixth Avenue. This 350-foot tower of wood and iron boasted a steam elevator that took you to the observation towers and the telescopes. You could see (*lower left*) the small wooden house that stood on the northwest corner of 42nd Street and Fifth Avenue. The big Croton distributing reservoir with its squat Egyptian walls faced Fifth Avenue from 42nd to 40th Streets (the Public Library is there now). The promenade around the top of the walls was a favorite place for New Yorkers to walk on Sunday afternoon just as today they walk around the reservoir in Central Park. Opposite was the Mount Croton Garden and beyond at 40th Street stood Croton Cottage, a popular roadhouse. At Madison Avenue and 37th Street were three identical brownstones—one still standing today, the former home of J. P. Morgan.

Museum of the City of New York

The Latting Observatory, between Fifth and Sixth Avenues, 42nd Street, 1853–1856.

Prominent in the foreground stands the Crystal Palace, at 42nd Street and Sixth Avenue, right next to the reservoir—and where Bryant Park is today. The Crystal Palace housed the first American World's Fair and gave New Yorkers an opportunity to inspect industrial and art exhibits, 6,000 in all, from Europe, the West Indies, Canada and the United States. The huge iron and glass building was opened in 1853 and burned to the ground in 1858. The Latting Observatory met the same fate in 1856.

Today as you look out over the same panorama from the observation roof at Rockefeller Center, seventy stories high, the only unchanged parts of the view are the contours along the distant horizon: the flat New Jersey shore at the right, the hills of Staten Island in the center, the Narrows and the Brooklyn waterfront with the Lower Bay beyond. New York's half million population has grown to 8,000,000, and Greater New York covers an area of 359 square miles. Instead of the 350-foot tower of the Latting Observatory, tallest building in the world a century ago, there looms up the Empire State Building (today's tallest), 1,250 feet high with a 222-foot television-sending tower atop that. In the left foreground is the Salmon Tower, replacing the small wooden house at Fifth Avenue and 42nd Street. The orderly rows of trees far below in Bryant Park stand on the spot where the Crystal Palace used to be. Church spires have all been swallowed up, houses have disappeared, even the streets themselves are blotted out. The mass of buildings has obliterated the pattern of yesterday. It's a new city indeed.

The RCA Building, sentinel of mid-Manhattan, 1953.

It is incredible to realize that, looking down from the RCA Building, 42nd Street can hardly be seen. Cutting a wide swath across the center of the island from river to river, it is a street of many interests, typical of the city itself in its variety and its throngs of people. In the foreground is the Hudson River.

Crystal Palace and
Latting Observatory.

People first came to 42nd Street in great numbers during the 1840's, attracted by the new Croton reservoir at Fifth Avenue. Then the Crystal Palace, opening in 1853 with its breath-taking displays, drew the people as did the later balls and fairs held there. Another place that interested them was the Latting Observatory with its superb view. After the Crystal Palace burned, the site was converted into a park again and the block opposite was soon lined with substantial homes, for this was an attractive location. It was in 1884 that the park was named for William Cullen Bryant. Today it remains an island of relative calm in the swirl of mid-Manhattan life. Office worker, shopper and lounger gratefully enjoy this patch of green. At the east end rise the book stacks of the Public Library whose walls with the small windows bring a fortress-like feeling of protection to the nearby park and the people sitting there.

Bryant Park, looking northeast from Sixth
Avenue toward 42nd Street.

Museum of the City of New York

Squatters living with their goats and pigs in tumbled-down shanties set among Manhattan's rocks were as typical of New York a century ago as are the skyscrapers today. Only a few blocks beyond the Crystal Palace, on 42nd Street between Second and Third Avenues, was this large settlement in the 1860's. Battling with their neighbors, battling with the authorities, the squatters gave way with the greatest reluctance to the demands of the growing city. And this was only the first step, for after the squatters were removed, came the task of leveling the rocks and, sometimes, the streets themselves, until the desired flatness had been achieved and another row of houses could go up. Today, within a stone's throw of that squatter settlement, rise some of New York's best known edifices: the Chrysler tower, its new, white annex, and on the south side of the street, the Daily News Building. With the brilliance of these towers, and the nearby United Nations Secretariat Building, 42nd Street holds its own against the beauty of a night view of lower Manhattan.

Looking west along 42nd Street from the Chanin Building, you can glimpse, past the Lincoln Building (*left*) and the Salmon Tower (*right*), the many-sided life of 42nd Street: first, Hudson River shipping; a small-business area; the theatrical district with its cheap movie houses and glittering Times Square; then the crossroads of 42nd Street and Fifth Avenue where, it is said, at some time every one will pass by.

Look toward the East River from the Chanin Building beyond the Grand Central Terminal area where will pass, during one year, as many people as there are in the whole United States. Walk on under New York's sole remaining Ele- vated, past the Daily News Building and the apartment houses of Tudor City, finally reach- ing the newest facet in the life of this street— the world home of the United Nations, over- looking the East River.

The United Nations Secretariat Building is not the first to dominate the East River shore. In 1823 George Youle erected a shot tower that was a landmark all through the nineteenth century. Here he carried on a thriving business making shot (the molten lead poured from the top of the tower becoming perfect balls by the time it dropped into the pool of water at the bottom of the tower). A little south of the tower (45th Street today) a military storehouse stood for many years. In 1775, when New York sorely needed ammunition in the early days of the Revolution, this was raided several times and British stores seized.

Old military storehouse, 45th Street and the East River, as it looked in 1852.

This East River shore was sprinkled with country houses, spacious and homey, with a splendid view. Then the land, divided into building lots, gave way to abattoirs, warehouses, powerhouses and tenements.

With the 1920's began the upswing. Tudor City, a $25,000,000 apartment house development, was built at 42nd Street; next, the Franklin D. Roosevelt Drive; and with the 1950's, the United Nations buildings.

United Nations, Assembly
Building, southern façade.

Eighteen acres of international territory in the heart of New York—this is
United Nations, N. Y., situated between First Avenue and the East River, from
42nd to 48th Streets. The ground was given by John D. Rockefeller, Jr., supple-
mented by land donated by the city to round out the plot and provide space for
driveways and gardens. The group of buildings offers both architecturally and
in interior layout and decoration a modern, breath-taking concept of design. The
dominating feature is the Secretariat Building, thirty-nine stories of marble and
glass. This was opened in August, 1950, and the low-domed General Assembly
Building in October, 1952. Connecting them is the Conference Building with
meeting rooms for the Security Council, the Trusteeship Council and the Eco-
nomic and Social Council. The United Nations buildings have become a mecca
for tourists. Hundreds crowd in daily to wander through the lobbies, join one
of the guided tours, and, whenever possible, visit a session of the Assembly or a
Council meeting. In the words of Dag Hammarskjold, Secretary-General of the
United Nations, "These buildings are the physical embodiment of your United
Nations, an organization whose aim is peace and freedom for all in a world of
equal rights for all."

United Nations, Secretariat
Building, western façade.

Hill Brothers, 213 Canal Street, 1870's.

Turning again to the people and how they live—their stores and markets, their homes and amusements—let's start back in the 1870's, when the main shopping center was along Broadway and Grand Street and many of today's names were already familiar: Lord and Taylor, Arnold Constable, Hearn, Tiffany, Brooks and Sloane. Women's clothes were mostly made at home or by local dressmakers, so there was a flourishing business in yard goods, ribbons, braid and laces. Millinery, too—hence such big establishments as Hill Brothers which sold only bonnet frames, hat shapes and trimmings. A few places like Lord and Taylor's were beginning to sell ready-made hats as well as the materials. With the introduction of ready-to-wear clothes came another innovation, women clerks.

Lord and Taylor's millinery department, Grand and Chrystie Streets, in the 1870's.

Characteristic of New York today are the huge department store with their amazing variety of stock and their aisles jammed with people who sometimes come many miles to buy in the big stores. It's hard to believe that Macy's, shown here, started as a small emporium on Sixth Avenue and 14th Street in 1858.

Many shoppers never leave their own neighborhood, preferring the security of a small local store where they know the proprietor. They like to handle the profusion of merchandise that swings overhead and is stacked on every available inch of space. Some storekeepers retain the flavor of their homeland but many others strive to become modern and meet the demands of a new generation.

The great question is: "Are they gonna buy?" These women are real shoppers, they know all the tricks. When you stop, slip your aching foot out of your shoe and prop your shopping bag between your feet for safety. The shiny black bag is the badge of the east side housewife, whether she is buying from pushcart, small shop or super-market, whether she finds bargains on outdoor counters or inside the shops.

Washington Market, Fulton to Vesey Streets, along the Hudson River, in 1853, before it became the largest wholesale produce market in the country.

Fulton Market, Fulton to Beekman Streets, along the East River, in 1878, before it developed into the largest wholesale fish market on the Atlantic coast.

A century ago people were buying much of their fresh food directly from the general markets. As time went on, markets began to specialize and turn to the wholesale trade. Now Fulton market is the largest fish market and Washington the largest produce center. Today the Washington wholesale area extends north from Vesey Street for more than a quarter of a mile, covering the blocks between West and Greenwich Streets. Here is sold a large proportion of the 12½ billion pounds of perishable food that comes into the city annually. Only within the modern market house itself at Vesey and Washington Streets do you find retail stalls. However, here you'll see all the variety of the old-time market— meats, cheeses, fish and vegetables—plus the imports unknown a century ago. No more pushcarts along the curbs, but attractive displays inside.

Depot of the New York and New Haven Railroad, 4th Avenue and 27th Street, 1860.

Train shed of the Grand Central Depot, 42nd Street and 4th Avenue, 1871.

Railroad travel commenced here in 1830 when the New York and Harlem ran horse-drawn cars over a route from Prince Street to 14th Street. By 1837 it was a full-fledged steam railroad. Next, the New York and New Haven Railroad organized in 1844 for the New England traffic and in 1857 the two lines built adjacent depots on 4th Avenue between 26th and 27th Streets. Meanwhile the Hudson River line, incorporated in 1846, laid tracks on 10th, 11th and 12th Avenues, and in 1869 consolidated with the New York Central. The pressure of the rapidly growing city led all three to build a Grand Central Depot in 1871.

Today's two great stations were built at almost the same time, the Pennsylvania (whose great glass-roofed concourse is shown above) in 1910, and the new Grand Central Terminal in 1913. Over 200,000 commuters pour through these stations daily as do a large proportion of the city's 13,000,000 annual visitors.

New York as seen from Weehawken, N. J., today.

New York as seen from Weehawken, N. J., 1820's.

There wasn't a single railroad in the country when this charming, almost idyllic, picture was drawn in the 1820's. To the artist, standing on Weehawken Heights, there was beauty in the broad sweep of the Hudson River and the low-lying island of Manhattan. To the railroader, the topography posed great problems: there wasn't enough space for freight yards on the island, so terminals would have to be constructed on the New Jersey shore. With this came the difficulty of getting the freight across the river to the city. Hence the great development of tracks, piers and warehouses where, by an intricate sorting process, freight cars are sent to various points for the transfer of cargoes to ocean freighters, to scows for local hauls, to car-floats which carry the loaded freight cars themselves, or to waterfront cargo terminal buildings.

Jacob Riis' own photograph of "Bandit's Roost" in Mulberry Street, about 1888.

New York never caught up with the problem of decent housing for the multitudes who poured in after 1840. People were packed into hastily built tenements and cheaply reconverted buildings. A competition for a well-designed tenement in 1879 only made matters worse by creating the "Dumb-bell Plan," with three-foot air shafts between houses and with windowless rooms. Jacob Riis aroused people with his photographs and descriptions, and the formation of the State Tenement Housing Commission helped. Plans for slum clearance and better housing slowly moved ahead. In 1934 the building of Knickerbocker Village, a private enterprise, wiped out a notorious "lung block" on Cherry Street, and the following year the first city housing project was opened: First Houses on Avenue A and 3rd Street.

From original negative by Jacob A. Riis, Museum of the City of New York

Pushcarts in Hester Street, about 1900.

Leonard Hassam Bogart Collection, Museum of the City of New York

In all older sections of Manhattan you find these typical tenements, six stories high, four flats to a floor, "railroad" layout of connecting rooms with no hall. Much worse were the ones with the toilets in the public hall, and the "dumb-bell" darkness. Fortunately, better housing is wiping these out rapidly.

A leather bucket and a wooden rattle made up the first fire equipment in New Amsterdam. The watchman, sounding the alarm with his rattle, brought the Dutchmen flying with their buckets to make a line from pump to blaze. Peter Stuyvesant, disturbed by the number of houses burned, appointed fire officials, wardens or inspectors who frequently fined the unfortunates who had been burned out. With the fine money the town bought hooks, ladders and more buckets. In 1731 the first fire engines arrived from England, two hand-pumpers about five feet high. A century later pumpers could throw water to the top of four- and five-story buildings (as high as was needed then) but it was still done by man-power—the same men who had hauled pumper and hose cart to the fire. The volunteer fire companies, each proud of its own outfit and jealous of the others, made one of the most colorful episodes in the city's history. Not until 1865 was there a paid city organization, the Metropolitan Fire District.

Daily News

In 1952 New York had 52,741 fires with a loss of $26,948,000, and 99.8% of these fires were extinguished "within the area involved upon arrival of the apparatus." Today's equipment includes water towers, smoke ejectors, air compressor units (to breach concrete), foam powder units (for oil fires) and fire boats.

Under the new city management all apparatus was horse-drawn, and steam engines began to replace hand-pumpers. Ask any old-timer about fire engines fifty years ago. What a sight *that* was, especially at night. Smoke belching forth, sparks flying, three horses galloping like mad, the heavy shining engine thundering over the Belgian blocks of the avenue.

One spectacular fire gutted the Equitable Building, 120 Broadway, on a freezing, windy January morning in 1912. There had been disastrous fires around Wall Street before. In 1776 one quarter of the city (the entire west side) had burned, and in 1835 and 1845, 700 and 300 buildings respectively were destroyed and the business section wiped out.

Row of brownstone fronts in West 127th Street.

Brownstone fronts sprang up all over the city in the latter half of the nineteenth century. With so much space available, builders could put up long rows of identical brownstone houses at prices suitable for the middle-income groups. These houses, found in all parts of town, were similar in layout: high front stoop, long narrow hall and stairs, long narrow parlor with long narrow windows. The dining-room in the rear was directly over the kitchen and the food was hauled up in a dumb-waiter. Upstairs the main bedrooms, front and rear, were connected by dressing-rooms with wash-basins and clothes closets. The small "hall bedroom" achieved dreary recognition in the later days when the brownstone front became a rooming house, a fate which has overtaken many today.

Before any buildings went up on a piece of property, there often were people living on it. These were the squatters who threw a shack together out of such odd pieces of building material as they could retrieve, and settled in among the hills and rocks with their children and animals. Here they lived in dirt and squalor as bad as that of their tenement house brethren, but it was the only solution that some of the immigrants could find for the problems presented by poverty and the dearth of living quarters. It has been estimated that during the 1880's about 5,000 squatters were living east of Central Park. By 1900 the march northward was bringing marble palaces and French chateaux into this area, and Fifth Avenue was soon lined with handsome homes. By 1950 many of the houses had been made over into small apartments, or had been torn down to make way for the luxurious apartment houses and hotels that now tower above the park.

Apartment houses, Central Park South.

J. Clarence Davies Collection, Museum of the City of New York

Apartments in New York were first known as French or Spanish flats because of their origin. One of the earliest was the Navarro located on Central Park South, near where Essex House and Hampshire House are today. In spite of the many changes in the city, the first apartment house still stands—the Rutherford-Stuyvesant at 142 East 18th Street, built in 1869. These early apartments, high-ceilinged and spacious, were well suited to the uncrowded, leisurely life of that period. Today's apartments, compact, with fewer and smaller rooms, are better equipped and reflect the efficiency and speed of life today.

A new city pattern, now very familiar, is the housing development: tall apartments, set at an angle, turn their brick faces toward the sun. A community within a community, they look quite out of place amid the neighboring hodgepodge of aging buildings. In the twenty years since 1935, when the first city housing project started, the number has grown amazingly. Now there are eighty-five developments completed or started in the five boroughs. In addition to the low-priced city projects, there are such private ventures as Parkchester in the Bronx, and the two shown here, Peter Cooper Village and Stuyvesant Town, extending from 23rd Street (*left*) to 14th Street (*right*) from First Avenue to the East River.

Greenwood Cemetery,
Brooklyn, 1847.

Even in death the people stay crowded together, huddled in the great cemeteries of Brooklyn and Queens, still under the shadow of the giants who towered over them in life. Greenwood, the oldest cemetery, was developed by a group of citizens who realized that interments could not continue in rapidly growing New York. They assembled land in Brooklyn near Fifth Avenue and 25th Street and opened the cemetery in 1840. Its well-planned landscaping attracted many visitors, who came from afar to drive along the winding roads of this beauty spot. Today there are twenty miles of road in the 478 acres, and over half a million interments have been made. Soon after Greenwood began, other cemeteries were laid out—Evergreen, Cypress Hills, Mount Olivet, Calvary. In Manhattan itself the small quiet cemeteries still attract the passers-by. Trinity's and St. Paul's are familiar to many, but less well known are the Marble Cemetery on East 2nd Street, the fragment of Shearith Israel's plot on West 11th Street near 6th Avenue, and oldest of all, the cemetery established by the Jewish people in 1656 at the Bowery near Chatham Square.

Typical cemetery in Brooklyn-
Queens area, 1953.

The changes of the years show up just as clearly in the heart of New York. "Mutiny on a Slave Ship," and a "Rendezvous in Gay Paree," all for fifteen cents —one of 42nd Street's bargains which are the sole attraction now of the once famous street of the the-atrical world. Today's legitimate theaters are scattered mostly between 43rd and 52nd Streets off Broadway which, too, has been taken over by the movies and the honky-tonk attractions. Day or night, however, natives and visitors crowd the streets.

Photograph by Byron, Museum of the City of New York

45th Street, west of Broadway. Hits of 1953.

New York's theater district is not hers alone, it is a recreation center claimed by the whole nation. The crowds moving up and down the street have come from all sections of the country and form a great part of the audience, be it a cheap movie or an expensive stage production. Sixty years ago, however, the theater had come to them—there were stock companies, road companies and vaudeville everywhere. Typical of that period was Tony Pastor "father of vaudeville." His final theater (1890) was located on 14th Street near Third Avenue, not far from Union Square.

Looking north from 43rd Street, Broadway and Seventh Avenue, 1905.

Theaters invaded the Broadway-42nd Street area at the turn of the century, and by 1905 included the Criterion, Republic, Lyric, Liberty, Hudson, Lyceum and the New York Theater. The Hotel Astor had opened in 1904 and the Times Building in 1905. These were the years, too, of Rector's and Shanley's restaurants, the Cadillac and Knickerbocker hotels. Nickelodeons were the popular movie places, offering one- and two-reel pictures at a nickel admission. The next few years would see the development of motion picture theaters with full-length programs: five- and six-reel features, serials, cartoons and newsreels. The opening of the Strand in 1914 introduced a new high in movie theater elegance, and from then on elaborate décor was in order. In 1926 the gigantic Roxy's was completed, and size as well as decoration became a requisite of motion picture palaces. Overhead, electric signs became brighter and bigger: the Corticelli kitten played with her spool of silk high above Broadway, and the Spearmint soldiers in the Wrigley advertisement went through their military drill. This was the Great White Way in earnest. Today it's a world of chromium, neon lights, cut-rates and crowds.

Looking north from 43rd Street, Broadway and Seventh Avenue, today.

Photograph by Byron, Museum of the City of New York

Madison Square Garden, built 1890, 4th Avenue and 26th Street.

Equally famous as an amusement center is Madison Square Garden. After Grand Central Terminal opened at 42nd Street, P. T. Barnum and several associates leased the old New York and New Haven depot at 26th Street and converted it into an auditorium. Every kind of spectacle went on there: boxing, revival meetings, walking races, balls, concerts and the circus. Gilmore's Band appeared and with it the name Gilmore's Garden—then the name became Madison Square Garden. In 1890 a new garden rose on the same site: a handsome, arcaded building with a tower copied after the Giralda in Spain and which held a theater, a concert hall and an auditorium seating 8,000 people. It housed horse shows, flower shows, political conventions, the circus and innumerable sports events. When "the Garden" left Madison Square it took the name along to the new site, 8th Avenue, 49th to 50th Street, where it opened in 1925. Here it offers the same varied fare in a larger arena where, for example, at the Louis-Walcott fight in 1947, over 18,000 watched the drama in that small lighted ring.

Madison Square Garden, built 1925, 8th Avenue and 50th Street.

Museum of the City of New York

Polo Grounds, Fifth
Avenue and 110th
Street, 1886.

The New-York Historical Society

Polo Grounds, home of the Giants, 155th Street and Harlem Driveway, today.

Or maybe you want to see a ball game—the Giants, for instance, in a night game up at the Polo Grounds near the Harlem River and 155th Street. This park, built in 1912, holds about 60,000 people and the Yankee Stadium just across the river is even larger. That was built in 1923. The third major league park, Ebbets Field, home of the Dodgers, is at Bedford Avenue and Sullivan Place in Brooklyn—that was built in 1912, too. Back in the 1880's the Polo Grounds wasn't so far uptown. You only had to go to 110th Street and Fifth Avenue, in the popular Harlem section. Even then baseball was well established, for in 1845 the Knickerbocker Baseball Club of New York was formally organized and in 1849 appeared in the first uniforms, suits of blue and white. The game turned professional in 1871 with the creation of the National Association. As for night baseball, the earliest game on record was played in 1880 and it was introduced in the major leagues in 1935.

"The steamboat excursions to Flushing and other landings on the Long Island shore are delightful during warm weather," recommended the 1876 guide book. New Yorkers were fortunate because, being "islanders," they had a wide choice of places to go. Fort Lee on the Jersey side made a popular short trip (the boat left from West 13th Street) and the long day trip to West Point and Newburgh was also highly praised. Long Branch on the New Jersey shore (reached by boat to Sandy Hook and then steam-cars) was a popular objective in the nineties because the president summered there. Most fun of all was the Iron Steamboat trip to Coney Island, Manhattan Beach and Rockaway. Down the harbor, through the Narrows, around to Coney, where you landed at the Iron Pier and ate at one of the restaurants located there, or on to Rockaway inlet. Everybody took a steamboat excursion in those days.

Plan an all-day boat excursion now and the chances are that you'll go up the Hudson on one of the big day liners, each deck filled with sightseers anxious for a chance to see the lofty Palisades, the wide stretch of Tappan Zee, Storm King Mountain and West Point. Perhaps you'll stop at one of the picnic grounds or recreation parks near the river's edge. Too bad the night boats have all gone. Whether you went to Albany or Troy, to New Haven or Hartford, to Fall River, Providence or Boston, you left the city during the late afternoon with time before darkness fell to enjoy the splendid skyline slipping by and to watch the many different kinds of ships that you passed on the way. To the young ones it seemed almost as good as a voyage on a transatlantic liner.

Excursion boat to Rockaway, 1878.

Up the Hudson by the Day-line, today.

Crowds at a side show, the Bowery, Coney Island, 1890's.

You took the Iron Steamboat to Coney or else the Culver Line's steam railroad. Coney Island was the place: people had been going there for years but now it was even better, there was more entertainment. Besides the ocean and the beach there was Surf Avenue with its pavilions and its beer gardens, where the waiters sang and somebody played a piano. Oh, yes, there were those new things called frankfurters, too. Then there was the Bowery, that extra street tucked in between Surf Avenue and the beach, where the side shows were, where "A Turkish Harem" reminded you that "Little Egypt" of the Chicago's World Fair had started a craze which spread far and wide. This was Coney in the nineties. In 1897 Steeplechase opened, the first of Coney's famous amusement parks and the only one still going today. East of Coney Island were Brighton Beach, Manhattan Beach and Sheepshead Bay with their comfortable wide-porched summer hotels, their race tracks, Diamond Jim Brady and Lillian Russell, and the magnificent displays of Pain's fireworks.

Photograph by Adolph Wittemann,
The Leonard Hassam Bogart Collection,
Museum of the City of New York

Thousands and thousands of lights. Every white and red tower of Luna Park was outlined with them. Was there ever anything more glorious than the night view from the top of the Shoot-the-Chute at Luna? Did you ever ride on the Circle Swing and the Dragon's Gorge there? And do you remember Dreamland that burned in 1911 after a spectacular start as an amusement park? Amusement parks . . . the Bowery . . . Feltman's . . . Ravenhall's . . . frankfurters . . . shoddy batn houses and dirty beaches . . . that was Coney Island before 1920.

With the coming of the subway in 1920 and the opening of the boardwalk in 1921, Coney was only a nickel away and the beach was more inviting than ever. The 100,000 who visited Coney on a summer Sunday in 1900 have become 1,000,000 today. There's more doing along the boardwalk, less along

Surf Avenue and the Bowery. Now it's the Parachute Jump, roller coasters, knishes and cotton candy. The music of the carousel is an almost forgotten sound. But the beach! On a summer week-end, it's crowded enough, but during a hot spell—let's see if we can find a square inch of sand to call our own.

The multitude of people crowding the beach is an appreciable fraction of New York's eight million citizens who, with the traditions of three centuries behind them, shape the city for future generations.

On guard over them all stands the Goddess of Liberty, against a background of star tracks, bringing her message of freedom which remains as steadfast in its orbit as do the stars in theirs.